Keto Desserts Cookbook #2019

Quick & Easy Recipes to Reset Your Body and Live a Healthy Life (Lose Weight, Balance Hormones, Boost Brain Health, and Reverse Disease)

Dr Anna Richouly

Readers acknowledge that the author is not engaging in the rendering of legal, financial, medical or professional advice.

By reading this document, the reader agrees that under no circumstances are we responsible for any losses, direct or indirect, which are incurred as a result of the use of information contained within this document, including, but not limited to, errors, omissions, or inaccuracies.

Table of contents

Chapter 1: Ketogenic Desserts Basics

Nothing can drive you crazier than stopping yourself from sweets and desserts when you have a sweet tooth. Well, these days many people cannot afford to have sugars in their meals, either due to risks of obesity, diabetes, and other health conditions. Where Ketogenic diet has been successful in claiming the prevention and cure of such ailments, it has also contributed well by providing low carb, no sugar dessert alternatives for all. Earlier, people used to either compromise on their health to eat delicious food or compromise on the taste to keep themselves healthy, but today ketogenic desserts have put those worries to an end. The immense variety of keto-Friendly ingredients have brought ease and comfort to the lives of every dieter.

To tap our memory lets go back into some basic details of the ketogenic diet. The idea is based on a diet which can cause ketosis in the body. That is only possible when we have a low carb and high-fat meal. Ketosis breaks fats and produces a high dose of energy and ketones; both are good for the human body. Keeping this concept in mind, the nutritionists have created an entire meal plan, and the ketogenic desserts form an important part of that plan. This cookbook is focused entirely on keto desserts in order to discover unique and interesting ways to introduce better flavors to the lives of all the dieters.

Sugar-Free Keto Dessert

Imagining a sugar free dessert does not come easy to the mind, as we always go for sugar to add the desired sweetness of every other dessert. Such sweetness can also be achieved without compromising your health now. Ketogenic desserts have brought the idea of the sugar-free meal into reality with several of their low carb alternatives. These recipes share the same aroma, flavors, and even the outlook, with other high carb desserts but they contain a significantly low amount of carbohydrates and a high dose of fats. Remember that the carbs should not exceed the 13-gram threshold. So the keto desserts maintain the taste within this range and provide all the delicious options. There are numerous ingredients that can be substituted to reduce the carb levels in the recipe. For instance, omitting sugars, high carb fruits, grains, legumes, and milk, and replace them with other plant-based low carb substitutes which are later discussed in this section in great detail. These desserts are not only suitable for people who are entirely following a ketogenic diet, but even other dieters can also switch to it for its amazing health benefits.

Ketogenic Substitutes for Desserts

1. Diary Vs. Non-Dairy Milk

When you analyze the nutritional content of animal milk, the ration between carbohydrates and fats is 5:1, which rightly indicates that cow, goat or any other animal milk is not keto friendly.   Rather than milk alone can drastically increase the carb levels in the ketogenic dessert. Since milk is an important part of every other dessert ingredients, it cannot be completely omitted. Though it can be replaced with other low carb alternatives which are equally rich and tasty and give a suitable consistency to different keto desserts.

1. Coconut milk
1. Almond Milk
2. Hazelnut milk
3. Cashew Milk
4. Macadamia Milk

5. Hemp Milk

Coconut and almond milk, are most commonly used milk substitutes for the ketogenic diet. It is because of the availability of these products in the market. Cashew milk is another great alternative which can even be prepared at home with its special recipe. Nuts are soaked and processed to obtain their liquid which highly nutritious.

2. Baking Flours

The ordinary baking flours are usually processed out of wheat or other grains and legumes. Since these sources are high in carbohydrates, their flours are also not suitable for ketogenic desserts. That is why all types of whole wheat flours, chickpea flour, self-rising flour, rice flour, etc. should be avoided and they all need to be replaced with other low carb alternatives including the following:

1. Coconut Flour
2. Almond flour
3. Other nut flours.

Dry nuts are used to obtain all those flours. Since nuts do not contain high doses of carbohydrates, the fine powder obtained out of them is therefore completely keto-friendly.

3. Dairy Items

Not all dairy products are full of carbohydrates as milk, there are several dairy items which are processed out of the milk, but they lose their carbohydrates in this process. This means that they are keto friendly and do not spike the level of glucose in the body whenever taken. Those dairy items include the following:

1. Cream cheese

1. Yogurt
2. Cheese
3. Butter
4. Cream
5. Eggs

When it comes to ketogenic desserts, these ingredients are most commonly used in making batters, frostings, and toppings.

4. Swerves

When it comes to ketogenic desserts, all-natural sugars are prohibited. Cane sugar, brown sugar, packed or processed sugar, table sugar, white sugar and other sweeteners like honey, molasses, sugar syrup, etc. are all your enemies when you are on a ketogenic diet. Simply cross these items off your grocery list to make your meal low carb. Luckily due to the immense popularity and use of the ketogenic diet, now there are several widely available keto specific sweeteners that can do the job and doesn't make your compromise on the flavors.

These artificial sweeteners add taste without adding the carb content. Each of them has its own intensity and texture, which should be kept into consideration while they are used. The table given in this section indicates the list of the ketogenic sweeteners along with their proportionate conversion to sugar in accordance with the level of sweetness.

- Swerve

Swerve is an artificial keto sweetener which comes in both the superfine and granulated texture. These forms help to add this substitute as per the desired consistency of the recipe.

- Stevia

Stevia is that substitute which is available in both the liquid and powdered forms. Use any of its forms as per the need of the recipe. It is about 200 times sweeter than ordinary table sugar. So, use the given table to convert the amount of sugar proportionately into stevia. Try to add it as per taste to avoid confusion.

- Erythritol

Just like swerve, Erythritol is another commonly used artificial sweetener, which is usually available in white powdered form, packed in a box. Use the following table to measure the equal amount of the erythritol carefully.

Table 1.1

Sugar	1 tsp	1 tbsp	1/4 cup	1/3 cup	1/2 cup	1 cup
Erythritol	1 1/4 tsp	1 Tbsp + 1 tsp	1/3 cup	1/3 cup + 2 Tbsp	2/3 cup	1 1/3 cup
Swerve	1 tsp	1 Tbsp	1/4 cup	1/3 cup	1/2 cup	1 cup
Stevia Extract	-	-	3/16 tsp	1/4 tsp	3/8 tsp	3/4 tsp
Liquid Stevia	3/8 tsp	3/8 tsp	1 1/2 tsp	2 tsp	3 tsp	2 Tbsp
Sweet Leaf Sweet Drops	-	1/8 tsp	1/2 tsp	2/3 tsp	1 tsp	2 tsp
Sukrin	1 tsp	1 Tbsp	1/4 cup	1/3 cup	1/2 cup	1 cup
Truvia	1/2 tsp	1 1/4 tsp	1 Tbsp + 2 tsp	2 Tbsp + 1 tsp	3 1/2 Tbsp	1/3 + 1 1/2 Tbsp
Pure Monk	-	-	1/6 tsp	1/4 tsp	1/3 tsp	2/3 tsp

Monk fruit	1 tsp	1 Tbsp	1/4 cup	1/3 cup	1/2 cup	1 cup
Monk Sweet	1/2 tsp	1 1/2 tsp	2 Tbsp	2 Tbsp + 2 tsp	1/4 cup	1/2 cup

Chapter2: Benefits of Ketogenic Desserts

The magic of the ketogenic diet unfolds in many ways. From mental health to physical strength, this meal plan offers prevention and cure to all the grave diseases prevalent today, through its low carb approach. Switching to no sugar diet is the most needed yet quite difficult part of this healthy lifestyle. Being a sweet tooth, you cannot simply hold up your cravings for sweets. Ketogenic desserts give such an alternative to all those sweet lovers. There are some other great advantages to those desserts:

- Great for Diabetic Patients

We know how diabetic patient struggle against their cravings for sweets and their unstable blood glucose levels. The ketogenic desserts not only satisfy their cravings but also tend to maintain their blood glucose level. These energizing desserts increase the energy levels of the body without spiking up the glucose levels as fats are consumed to obtain energy.

- Reduces Obesity

Sugary desserts are equal to the great number of Carbohydrates which is directly linked to obesity. Excess carbs are never consumed or released out of the body, rather they store somewhere inside and cause obesity, reduced pH levels, and other several complications. Ketogenic diets prevent the chances of obesity and helps in weight reduction.

- Lasting Energy Boots

Ketogenic desserts are a source of a good amount of fats, and they all contribute to the process of ketosis, that means the breakdown of fat molecules. Each molecule breaks to released three-time greater energy than the same amount of carbohydrates. This why fat loaded desserts provide long-lasting energy boosts.

- Accelerates the Metabolism

Carb-rich desserts often make us hyperactive or too lethargic after some time. This is because the energy boost is temporary and drains the body faster than ever. Ketosis, on the other hand, released energy gradually without creating a spike or hike, which progressively accelerates the rate of metabolism.

- Mental Strength

Patients suffering from Epilepsy or Alzheimer can take the most benefit out of ketogenic desserts, as they can improve their mental conditions significantly. Ketosis is the mechanism which detoxifies the brain cells and nourishes them with a gradual supply of energy and ketones.

- Amazing Taste

Cutting sugar out of the desserts is no fun for anyone. No one would want to choose tasteless food when they are given open choices. Ketogenic desserts give the people enough ideas or range of recipes which enable them to enjoy all the sweetness of life without compromising their health goals.

Chapter 3: Tips

Here come a few of the important tips which are crucial to remember while opting for ketogenic desserts:

1. Once you opt for a ketogenic lifestyle, start thinking and acting keto. This means plan everything according to your diet. Stuff your kitchen and pantry with keto specific ingredients.

2. Sugar substitution should be proportionate while making a ketogenic dessert. That means add the swerve as per its own intensity of sweetness, not proportionately equal to the amount of sugar usually used.

3. Chocolate cannot be avoided when it comes to desserts, but for a ketogenic diet, sugar-free chocolate is the only option we can pursue.

4. All the animal-based milk whether it's the cow milk or goat milk etc. should be avoided and they all need to be replaced with plant-based milk. Remember to use the plant-based substitution while considering their taste and consistency.

5. A good way to drastically increase the levels of fat in a ketogenic dessert is to add creamy, rich ingredients like cream cheese, cheese, yogurt, heavy cream, whipped cream, etc.

6. Fruits that are high in carbohydrates should not be added to the desserts in any form, whether pureed or whole. Oranges, apples, pineapples, watermelon, etc. are all high carb fruits.

7. Compared to other high carb fruits, berries are quite low on carbohydrates, and they make a suitable fit for a ketogenic diet. You can use them in any way possible.

8. Grain and legumes are strictly forbidden on the ketogenic diet, so don't go near the products processed out of them.

Chapter4: Cake Recipes

Lemon Coconut Cake

Prep Time: 15 minutes

Cooking Time: 45 minutes

Serving: 6

Ingredients:

Coconut Cake

- 1/2 cup coconut flour
- 5 eggs
- 1/4 cup erythritol
- 1/2 cup butter melted
- 1/2 lemon juiced
- 1/2 tsp lemon zest
- 1/2 tsp xanthan gum
- 1/2 tsp salt

Icing

- 1 cup cream cheese
- 3 tbsp powdered erythritol
- 1 tsp vanilla essence
- 1/2 tsp lemon zest

Method:

1. Separate egg yolks from egg whites.
2. Beat the egg whites in an electric mixer until peaks are formed.
3. Add the remaining ingredients in the egg yolk bowl.
4. Fold in the egg whites gently and mix until well incorporated.
5. Spread this batter in a greased loaf pan of 9x5 inches.

6. Bake it for 45 minutes at 335 degrees F.
7. Meanwhile, beat all the ingredients for cream cheese frosting in the electric mixer.
8. Once the cake is baked, allow it cool on wire rack.
9. Spread the frosting over the cake.
10. Refrigerate for 4 hours then slice to serve.

Nutritional Information per Serving:

- Calories 173
- Total Fat 16.2 g
- Saturated Fat 9.8 g
- Cholesterol 100 mg
- Total Carbs 9.4 g
- Sugar 0.2 g
- Fibre 1 g
- Sodium 42 mg
- Potassium 43 mg
- Protein 3.3 g

Keto Butter Cake

Prep Time: 15 minutes

Cooking Time: 35 minutes

Serving: 8

Ingredients:

- 3 tbsp coconut flour
- 1/4 cup powdered erythritol
- 1 tsp baking powder
- 1 tbsp gelatine
- 8 tbsp butter, room temperature
- 1/2 tsp vanilla essence
- 2 large eggs, room temperature

Top Layer

- 8 tbsp butter, room temperature
- 8 oz cream cheese, room temperature
- 1/4 cup powdered erythritol
- 1/2 tsp vanilla essence
- 50 drops liquid stevia
- 2 large eggs, room temperature

Method:

1. Let your oven preheat at 350 degrees F.
2. Grease an 8-inch baking pan with coconut oil.

Bottom Layer

3. Whisk eggs with butter, vanilla essence in an electric mixer.
4. Stir in erythritol, coconut flour, baking, and gelatin.
5. Mix well and set this batter aside.

Top Layer

6. Beat butter with cream cheese in another bowl using a hand mixer.
7. Whisk in eggs, vanilla essence, stevia, and erythritol.
8. Mix well and set this batter aside.

Cake

9. Add the bottom layer batter to the prepared pan.
10. Pour the top layer batter over it and spread it evenly.
11. Bake the cake for 35 minutes in the preheated oven.
12. Allow the cake to cool at room temperature.
13. Slice and serve.

Nutritional Information per Serving:

- Calories 251
- Total Fat 24.5 g
- Saturated Fat 14.7 g
- Cholesterol 165 mg
- Total Carbs 4.3 g
- Sugar 0.5 g
- Fiber 1 g
- Sodium 142 mg
- Potassium 80 mg
- Protein 5.9 g

Caramel Cake

Prep Time: 15 minutes

Cooking Time: 30 minutes

Serving: 6

Ingredients:

- 2 1/2 cups almond flour
- 3/4 cup almond milk
- 1/4 cup protein powder (without flavour)
- 1 tbsp baking powder
- 1/2 cup butter, melted
- 1/4 cup coconut flour
- 2/3 cup swerve
- 4 large eggs
- 1 tsp vanilla essence
- 1/2 tsp salt
- 2 batches sugar-free caramel sauce

Method:

Cake

1. Let your oven preheat at 325 degrees F. Grease 2- 8-inch baking pan with cooking oil.
2. Layer these pans with parchment paper and set them aside.
3. Mix both flours, protein, salt, and baking powder in a medium bowl.
4. Mix and beat butter with sweetener in a mixer until fluffy.
5. Whisk in all eggs one by one and vanilla.
6. Now stir in the coconut flour mix and coconut milk into the egg's mixture.
7. Divide this batter into the two pans. Bake them for 25 minutes.
8. Allow the baked cake to cool on wire rack.

Caramel Glaze

9. Cook the sugar-free caramel sauce in a saucepan until it bubbles.
10. Remove the glaze from the heat and allow it to cool.
11. Place on the cake over a plate and top it with 1/3 caramel sauce.
12. Spread the prepared glaze evenly and allow it to sit for 10 minutes.
13. Now place the second cake over it and pour the remaining caramel sauce on top.
14. Slice and serve.

Nutritional Information per Serving:

- Calories 264
- Total Fat 23.4 g
- Saturated Fat 11.7 g
- Cholesterol 135 mg
- Total Carbs 2.5 g
- Sugar 12.5 g
- Fiber 1 g
- Sodium 112 mg
- Potassium 65 mg
- Protein 7.9 g

Chocolate Cake in a Mug

Prep Time: 15 minutes

Cooking Time: 4 minutes

Serving: 2

Ingredients:

- ¼ teaspoon vanilla essence
- 1 ½ tablespoons swerve
- 2 tablespoons almond flour
- 1 large egg
- 2 tablespoons butter, salted
- 2 tablespoons cocoa powder, sugar free
- ½ teaspoon baking powder
- 2 teaspoons coconut flour

Method:

1. Melt butter in a mug in a microwave by heating for 20 seconds.
2. Add swerve and cocoa powder to the butter, and mix well in a bowl.
3. Stir in almond flour, coconut flour, vanilla, and baking powder.
4. Once the batter is smooth, divide the batter into two greased ramekins.
5. Cook the batter for 75 seconds in the microwave on high heat.
6. Beat whipped cream until foamy.
7. Top the cakes with this cream.
8. Serve.

Nutritional Information per Serving:

- Calories 359
- Total Fat 34 g
- Saturated Fat 10.3 g
- Cholesterol 112 mg
- Total Carbs 8.5 g

- Sugar 2 g
- Fiber 1.3 g
- Sodium 92 mg
- Potassium 59 mg
- Protein 7.5 g

Vanilla Berry Mug Cake

Prep Time: 5 minutes

Cooking Time: 1 minute

Serving: 1

Ingredients:

- 1 tbsp butter melted
- 2 tbsp cream cheese full fat
- 2 tbsp coconut flour
- 1 tbsp granulated swerve
- 1 tsp vanilla essence
- 1/4 tsp baking powder
- 1 egg medium
- 6 frozen raspberries

Method:

1. Beat butter with cream cheese in a mug.
2. Heat this mixture in the microwave for 20 seconds on High temperature.
3. Stir in coconut flour, baking powder, sweetener, and vanilla.
4. Mix well and whisk in the egg.
5. Once smooth, top the batter with 6 berries.
6. Cook the batter for 1 minute and 20 seconds on high temperature in the microwave.
7. Serve.

Nutritional Information per Serving:

- Calories 307
- Total Fat 29 g
- Saturated Fat 14g
- Cholesterol 111 mg
- Total Carbs 7 g

- Sugar 1 g
- Fiber 3 g
- Sodium 122 mg
- Potassium 78 mg
- Protein 6 g

Keto Carrot Cake Recipe

Prep Time: 15 minutes

Cooking Time: 20 minutes

Serving: 8

Ingredients:

cream cheese icing

- 8 oz cream cheese, softened
- 1/2 cup butter, softened
- 1/2 cup powdered Erythritol
- 1 tsp vanilla essence
- 2 tbsp heavy cream

carrot cake layers

- 5 eggs
- 3/4 cup erythritol
- 2 tsp vanilla essence
- 14 tbsp butter
- 1/4 cup shredded coconut
- 1/4 tsp salt
- 1/2 cup coconut flour
- 1 3/4 cup almond flour
- 2 tsp baking powder
- 1 1/2 tsp cinnamon ground
- 1 1/4 cup shredded carrots

Method:

cream cheese icing

1. Beat butter with cream cheese in a mixer for 2 minutes.
2. Add sweetener and beat again for 2 minutes.

3. Stir in 1 tbsp heavy cream and vanilla. Beat until the batter is thick.

carrot cake layers

4. Let your oven preheat at 350 degrees F.
5. Layer 2-8-inch baking pan with wax paper and greased them with cooking spray.
6. Beat eggs with erythritol in an electric mixer for 5 minutes until fluffy.
7. Stir in vanilla and beat again.
8. Mix both the flours with cinnamon, salt, and baking powder in a suitable bowl.
9. Add this ingredient to the egg mixture and mix well until smooth.
10. Fold in carrots and melted butter. Mix well gently.
11. Divide the carrot batter into two pans and bake them for 30 minutes.
12. Allow them to cool for 15 minutes on the wire rack.

To Assemble

13. Place on the cake on a plate and spread half of the icing over it evenly.
14. Place the other cake on top and spread the remaining icing on top.
15. Garnish with coconut shreds.
16. Refrigerate the cake for 30 minutes.
17. Slice and serve.

Nutritional Information per Serving:

- Calories 336
- Total Fat 34.5 g
- Saturated Fat 21.4 g
- Cholesterol 139 mg
- Total Carbs 9.1 g
- Sugar 0.2 g
- Fiber 1.1 g
- Sodium 267 mg
- Potassium 121 mg
- Protein 5.1 g

Lemon Custard Cake

Prep Time: 15 minutes

Cooking Time: 70 minutes

Serving: 8

Ingredients:

- 5 eggs, room temperature, whites separated from yolks
- 1 teaspoon vanilla essence
- 2/3 cup powdered erythritol
- 1/2 cup butter, unsalted, melted
- 1 cup superfine blanched almond flour
- 1/4 cup coconut flour
- 1 3/4 cup almond milk
- 1/4 cup lemon juice
- 2 tablespoons grated lemon zest

Method:

1. Let your oven preheat at 325 degrees F.
2. Layer an 8-inch baking dish with parchment paper.
3. Beat all the egg whites in an electric mixer until fluffy and set it aside.
4. Whisk egg yolks with sweeteners with a mixer until pale in color.
5. Stir in vanilla and melted butter.
6. Beat the mixture until smooth.
7. Add both flours, lemon zest, and juice, almond milk while beating the mixture slowly.
8. Finally, fold in the egg whites and mix gently.
9. Spread this batter in the baking dish and bake it for 70 minutes.
10. Allow the cake to cool then refrigerate for 2 hours.
11. Garnish with powder erythritol.
12. Slice and serve.

Nutritional Information per Serving:

- Calories 267
- Total Fat 44.5 g
- Saturated Fat 17.4 g
- Cholesterol 153 mg
- Total Carbs 8.4 g
- Sugar 2.3 g
- Fiber 1.3 g
- Sodium 217 mg
- Potassium 101 mg
- Protein 3.1 g

Chapter5: Keto bar Recipes

Homemade Keto Bars

Prep Time: 15 minutes

Cooking Time: 20 minutes

Serving: 4

Ingredients:

- 3/4 cup raw coconut meat
- 1/3 cup sugar free bakers' chocolate
- 2 tsp unflavoured protein powder
- 2.25 tbsp butter
- 1.5 tbsp water
- 3/4 tbsp heavy whipping cream
- Erythritol, to taste
- 35 drops liquid stevia

Method:

1. Put all the bar ingredients in a food processor.
2. Pulse the processor to blend the ingredients well.
3. Divide this mixture into the bar molds.
4. Bake them for 20 minutes at 250 degrees F.
5. Allow them to cool.
6. Serve.

Nutritional Information per Serving:

- Calories 316
- Total Fat 30.9 g
- Saturated Fat 8.1 g
- Cholesterol 0 mg

- Total Carbs 8.3 g
- Sugar 1.8 g
- Fiber 3.8 g
- Sodium 8 mg
- Potassium 87 mg
- Protein 6.4 g

Peanut Butter Bars

Prep Time: 15 minutes

Cooking Time: 0 minute

Serving: 8

Ingredients:

- Peanut Butter Filling:
- ½ cup smooth all-natural peanut butter
- 4 tbsp butter, melted
- 4 tbsp granulated erythritol
- 5 tbsp finely ground almond flour
- 1 tsp sugar-free vanilla essence

Coating

- 2.50 oz (approx.) sugar-free chocolate
- chopped peanuts for decoration

Method:

1. Combine all the filling ingredients in a suitable bowl until smooth.
2. Divide this filling into the silicone molds.
3. Place the silicon molds in the freezer for 30 minutes.
4. Meanwhile, chocolate in a double boiler.
5. Pour this melted chocolate over frozen filling bars and return the molds to the freezer.
6. Garnish the bars with chopped nuts.
7. Serve.

Nutritional Information per Serving:

- Calories 282
- Total Fat 25.1 g
- Saturated Fat 8.8 g

- Cholesterol 100 mg
- Total Carbs 9.4 g
- Sugar 0.7 g
- Fiber 3.2 g
- Sodium 117 mg
- Potassium 59 mg
- Protein 8 g

Keto Almond Milk Bars

Prep Time: 15 minutes

Cooking Time: 32 minutes

Serving: 8

Ingredients:

Crust

- 1 large egg
- 1 cup almond flour
- 1/4 teaspoon salt
- 2 tablespoons butter, unsalted

Condensed Milk

- Pinch of salt
- 1/2 cup heavy cream
- 1/2 cup Swerve
- 1/2 cup butter, unsalted
- 1 teaspoon vanilla essence

Top Layer

- 1 cup sugar free shredded coconut
- 9 oz sugar free Chocolate Chips
- 1 cup pecan, chopped

Method:

For the crust

1. Let your oven preheat at 300 degrees F.
2. Add and mix all the crust ingredients in a bowl until it forms a dough ball.
3. Spread this dough in an 8-inch baking pan and poke holes in it using a fork.
4. Bake the dough crust for 20 minutes until golden.

For the condensed milk:

5. Mix and heat all the condensed milk ingredients in a cooking pot.
6. Let it boil for 5 minutes with constant stirring.
7. Turn off the heat once this mixture thickens.

To assemble:

8. Toss pecan, chopped with chocolate chips and coconut.
9. Spread this mixture over the baked crust then pour the condensed milk over it.
10. Bake again for 7 minutes.
11. Refrigerate it for 1 hour.
12. Slice into small bars.
13. Serve.

Nutritional Information per Serving:

- Calories 358
- Total Fat 35.2 g
- Saturated Fat 15.2 g
- Cholesterol 69 mg
- Total Carbs 7.4 g
- Sugar 1.1 g
- Fiber 3.5 g
- Sodium 178 mg
- Potassium 114 mg
- Protein 5.5 g

Keto Coconut Bars

Prep Time: 15 minutes

Cooking Time: 0 minute

Serving: 6

Ingredients:

- 3 cups desiccated coconut sugar free
- 1/3 cup coconut cream
- 1/2 cup sugar-free syrup
- 4 tbsp coconut oil
- 1 oz sugar-free chocolate minimum

Method:

1. Add everything to a blender and blend them together on high speed.
2. Layer an 8x5 inch baking pan with wax paper.
3. Spread the coconut mixture into the prepared pan.
4. Press the mixture with your hand to smoothen out the surface.
5. Refrigerate this mixture for 15 minutes.
6. Slice it into square pieces.
7. Add chocolate to a bowl and melt it in the microwave.
8. Drizzle the melted chocolate over the coconut bars.
9. Return the bars to your refrigerator for 10 minutes.
10. Serve.

Nutritional Information per Serving:

- Calories 214
- Total Fat 19 g
- Saturated Fat 5.8 g
- Cholesterol 15 mg
- Total Carbs 6.5 g
- Sugar 1.9 g

- Fiber 2.1 g
- Sodium 123 mg
- Potassium 114 mg
- Protein 6.5 g

Samoa Cookie Bars

Prep Time: 15 minutes

Cooking Time: 30 minutes

Serving: 6

Ingredients:

Crust

- 1/4 cup swerve
- 1 1/4 cups almond flour
- 1/4 tsp salt
- 1/4 cup butter, melted

filling and drizzle

- 2 tbsp butter, melted
- 4 ounces sugar-free chocolate, diced

caramel filling

- 3 tbsp butter
- 1/4 cup swerve brown
- 3/4 cup heavy whipping cream
- 1 1/2 cups shredded coconut
- 1/4 cup mocha sweet
- 1/2 tsp vanilla essence
- 1/4 tsp salt

Method:

Crust

1. Let your oven preheat at 325 degrees F.
2. Mix almond flour with salt and sweetener in a medium bowl.
3. Stir in melted butter then spread this mixture in an 8-inch baking pan.

4. Press the mixture into the pan and bake it for 18 minutes.

Chocolate Filling/Drizzle

5. Melt chocolate with coconut oil in a glass bowl by heating in a microwave for 30 seconds.
6. Spread half of that melted chocolate over the baked crust.

Coconut Filling

7. Add coconut to a skillet and toast it until golden brown.
8. Melt butter in a saucepan with sweeteners.
9. Cook this mixture for 5 minutes until golden.
10. Remove it from the heat then stir in salt, cream, and vanilla.
11. Cook this mixture until it bubbles.
12. Gently stir in toasted coconut.
13. Add this mixture into the crust and allow it to cool for 1 hour.
14. Cut it into small squares.
15. Drizzle the remaining chocolate over them.
16. Serve.

Nutritional Information per Serving:

- Calories 313
- Total Fat 28.4 g
- Saturated Fat 12.1 g
- Cholesterol 27 mg
- Total Carbs 9.2 g
- Sugar 3.1 g
- Fiber 4.6 g
- Sodium 39 mg
- Potassium 185 mg
- Protein 8.1 g

Almond Butter Bars

Prep Time: 15 minutes

Cooking Time: 27 minutes

Serving: 6

Ingredients:

- 1 cup raw almonds, chopped
- 1 cup slivered almonds
- 1 cup sugar free coconut flakes, tightly packed
- 1 large egg
- 4 tbsp monk fruit
- 2 tbsp almond butter
- 1 tbsp coconut oil
- 3/4 tsp sea salt
- 1/4 cup stevia sweetened chocolate chips

Method:

1. Let your oven preheat at 375 degrees F. Layer an 8-inch pan with wax paper.
2. Spread chopped almond, coconut flakes and slivered almonds on separate baking sheets.
3. Toast the chopped almonds for 12 minutes, slivered almonds for 5 minutes and coconut shreds for 4 minutes.
4. Whisk egg with monk fruit in a suitable bowl.
5. Melt almond butter with coconut oil in a small bowl by heating in a microwave for 30 seconds.
6. Add this butter into the egg mixture then mix well.
7. Toss in all the nuts, salt, and coconut. Then stir in chocolate chips.
8. Add this mixture to the pan and press it firmly.
9. Bake the batter for 15 minutes at 350 degrees F.
10. Allow it to cool the slice.
11. Serve.

Nutritional Information per Serving:

- Calories 220
- Total Fat 20.1 g
- Saturated Fat 7.4 g
- Cholesterol 132 mg
- Total Carbs 63 g
- Sugar 0.4 g
- Fiber 2.4 g
- Sodium 157 mg
- Potassium 42 mg
- Protein 6.1 g

Keto Protein Bar

Prep Time: 10 minutes

Cooking Time: 0 minute

Serving: 6

Ingredients:

- 1 cup of nut butter
- 4 tbsps. of coconut oil (melted)
- 2 scoops of vanilla protein
- 10-15 drops of vanilla stevia
- ½ tsp of pink salt

Optional

- 4 tbsps. of sugar-free chocolate chips
- 1 tsp of cinnamon

Method:

1. Toss all the ingredients together in a suitable bowl.
2. Spread this mixture into a loaf pan.
3. Place the pan in the freezer then cut it into small bars.
4. Serve.

Nutritional Information per Serving:

- Calories 179
- Total Fat 15.7 g
- Saturated Fat 8 g
- Cholesterol 0 mg
- Total Carbs 4.8 g
- Sugar 3.6 g
- Fiber 0.8 g
- Sodium 43 mg

- Potassium 15 mg
- Protein 5.6 g

Keto Chocolate Bar

Prep Time: 15 minutes

Cooking Time: 0 minute

Serving: 6

Ingredients:

- 3 oz Cocoa butter
- 2 1/2 oz Sugar free baking chocolate
- 6 tbsp erythritol powder
- 2 tbsp Inulin
- 1/4 tsp Sunflower lecithin
- 1/8 tsp Sea salt
- 1 tsp Vanilla essence

Method:

1. Melt chocolate with cocoa butter in a double boiler on low heat.
2. Mix chocolate mixture with erythritol in a saucepan.
3. Stir in inulin, salt and sunflower lecithin.
4. Heat this mixture until smooth then turn off the heat.
5. Stir in vanilla essence and mix well.
6. Divide this mixture into a bar mold tray.
7. Place the bar tray in the refrigerator for 30 minutes.
8. Serve.

Nutritional Information per Serving:

- Calories 331
- Total Fat 32.9 g
- Saturated Fat 6.1 g
- Cholesterol 10 mg
- Total Carbs 9.1 g
- Sugar 2.8 g

- Fiber 0.8 g
- Sodium 18 mg
- Potassium 37 mg
- Protein 4.4 g

Chapter6: Pie and Tart Recipes

Low Carb Samoa Pie

Prep Time: 15 minutes

Cooking Time: 0 minute

Serving: 8

Ingredients:

Chocolate Crust

- 1/2 cup sunflower seeds raw, unsalted
- 1/2 cup sugar free cocoa powder
- 1/2 cup coconut flour
- 1/2 cup Swerve
- 1/2 tsp salt
- 8 tbsp butter soft

Filling

- 16 ounces heavy whipping cream
- 1 tsp vanilla liquid stevia
- 8 ounces cream cheese softened
- Topping
- 1/2 cup Coconut flakes sugar free, toasted
- 2 ounces my Microwave Salted Caramel Sauce
- 2 ounces Sugar-Free Chocolate Chips
- 3 tsp butter

Method:

1. Add and blend all the ingredients for the crust in a food processor.
2. Pulse the processor to blend everything together until smooth.
3. Spread this mixture into 9-inch pie pan and press it down. Set it aside.

4. Beat heavy cream with stevia and vanilla in a bowl.
5. Whisk the cream cheese in an electric mixer and stir in cream mixture.
6. Mix well then spread this filling into the pie crust.
7. Toss coconut flakes in a caramel sauce to prepare the topping.
8. Drizzle melted chocolate and caramel sauce mixture over the filling.
9. Refrigerate the pie for 3 hours.
10. Slice and serve.

Nutritional Information per Serving:

- Calories 190
- Total Fat 17.25 g
- Saturated Fat 7.1 g
- Cholesterol 20 mg
- Total Carbs 5.5 g
- Sugar 2.8 g
- Fiber 3.8 g
- Sodium 28 mg
- Potassium 47 mg
- Protein 3 g

Strawberry Cream Pie

Prep Time: 15 minutes

Cooking Time: 2 minutes

Serving: 3

Ingredients:

Shortbread Crust:

- 1 1/2 cups almond flour
- 1/4 cup powdered Swerve Sweetener
- 1/4 tsp salt
- 1/4 cup butter melted

Strawberry Cream Filling:

- 1 cup heavy whipping cream
- 1 1/2 cups fresh strawberries, chopped
- 1/4 cup water
- 2 1/2 tsp gelatine, grass fed
- 1/2 cup powdered Swerve Sweetener
- 3/4 tsp vanilla essence
- whipped cream for serving

Method:

1. Mix almond flour with salt and sweetener in a medium bowl.
2. Whisk in melted butter and mix well to form a coarse mixture.
3. Spread this mixture in a pie plate.
4. Spread the crust mixture into the plate and press it firmly.
5. Freeze this crust until the filling is prepared.

Strawberry Cream Filling:

6. Puree the strawberries in a blender or food processor with water.

7. Cook this puree with gelatine in a saucepan on low heat.
8. Bring it to a low simmer then turn off the heat. Allow it to cool for 20 minutes.
9. Beat cream with vanilla essence and sweetener in a suitable bowl.
10. Stir in strawberry mixture and mix well until smooth.
11. Spread this mixture into the frozen crust.
12. Refrigerate this pie for 3 hours.
13. Garnish with whipped cream and berries.
14. Serve.

Nutritional Information per Serving:

- Calories 321
- Total Fat 12.9 g
- Saturated Fat 5.1 g
- Cholesterol 17 mg
- Total Carbs 8.1 g
- Sugar 1.8 g
- Fiber 0.4 g
- Sodium 28 mg
- Potassium 137 mg
- Protein 5.4 g

Keto Blueberry Pie

Prep Time: 15 minutes

Cooking Time: 25 minutes

Serving: 8

Ingredients:

Crust

- 1/2 tablespoon water
- ½ cup butter, unsalted and melted
- 2 large eggs
- ¼ teaspoon salt
- ¾ cup coconut flour
- 1/8 teaspoon baking powder

Filling

- 1 tablespoons swerve
- 3/4 cup blueberries
- 8-ounce cream cheese

Method:

Crust Instructions

1. Prepare the crust dough by mixing all of the crust ingredients.
2. Divide this dough into two equal halves.
3. Roll both the halves into two-6-inch round sheets.
4. Place one sheet in a greased 6-inch pie plate and set the pan aside.

Pie Instructions

5. Let your oven preheat at 350 degrees F.
6. Spread cream cheese over the base layer of the crust.
7. Mix blueberries with 2 tbsp sweeteners in a bowl.

8. Spread this berry mixture over the cream cheese layer.
9. Place the other sheet of the dough on top of the filling.
10. Press and pinch the dough around the edges to seal the pie.
11. Bake the pie for 25 minutes in the preheated oven.
12. Allow the baked pie to cool at room temperature.
13. Slice and serve.

Nutritional Information per Serving:

- Calories 236
- Total Fat 21.5 g
- Saturated Fat 15.2 g
- Cholesterol 54 mg
- Total Carbs 7.6 g
- Sugar 1.4 g
- Fiber 3.8 g
- Sodium 21 mg
- Potassium 41 mg
- Protein 4.3 g

Keto Cheesecake Tarts

Prep Time: 15 minutes

Cooking Time: 20 minutes

Serving: 8

Ingredients:

Crust

- 3 tbsp butter, melted
- ¾ cup almond flour

Filling

- 12 oz. cream cheese, room temperature
- 1 egg
- ¼ cup erythritol
- 1 tsp vanilla essence
- 1 tbsp fresh lemon juice
- ¼ tsp salt
- Toppings
- ¼ cup sugar-free strawberry jam
- ¼ cup blueberries

Method:

1. Let your oven preheat at 350 degrees F.
2. Mix melted butter with almond flour in a bowl until it forms a coarse mixture.
3. Layer a muffin tray with cupcake liners and press 2 tsps of this mixture in the muffin cups.
4. Bake these crusts for 8 minutes in the preheated oven until golden.
5. Beat cream cheese in an electric mixer.
6. Add all the remaining filling ingredients and continue beating.
7. Divide this filling in the baked crusts.

8. Bake again for 20 minutes. Allow the cakes to cool.
9. Top them with jam and berries.
10. Refrigerate well then serve.

Nutritional Information per Serving:

- Calories 367
- Total Fat 35.1 g
- Saturated Fat 10.1 g
- Cholesterol 12 mg
- Total Carbs 8.9 g
- Sugar 3.8 g
- Fiber 2.1 g
- Sodium 48 mg
- Potassium 87 mg
- Protein 6.3 g

Dark Chocolate Tart

Prep Time: 15 minutes

Cooking Time: 27 minutes

Serving: 6

Ingredients:

Crust

- 6 tbsp coconut flour
- 2 tbsp erythritol
- 4 tbsp butter, melted
- 2 4-inch tart pans
- 1 large egg

Filling

- 1 large egg
- 2 oz sugar free chocolate, shredded
- 1/2 cup heavy whipping cream
- 30 drops liquid stevia
- 1/4 cup erythritol powder
- 1 oz cream cheese

Method:

1. Let your oven preheat at 350 degrees F.
2. Mix all the crust ingredients in a mixing bowl.
3. Divide this mixture into 4 tart pans and press it well.
4. Poke, some holes in the crust, then bake each for 12 minutes.
5. Allow these tart crusts to cool until the filling is ready.
6. Warm the cream up in a saucepan then pour it into a jar.
7. Add chopped chocolate and blend well using a hand blender.
8. Stir in stevia, erythritol, egg and cream cheese. Blend well until smooth.

9. Divide this filling into the baked crusts and return them to the oven.
10. Bake them for 15 minutes at 325 degrees F.
11. Allow them to cool then refrigerate for 2 hours.
12. Serve.

Nutritional Information per Serving:

- Calories 175
- Total Fat 16 g
- Saturated Fat 2.1 g
- Cholesterol 0 mg
- Total Carbs 2.8 g
- Sugar 1.8 g
- Fiber 0.4 g
- Sodium 8 mg
- Potassium 81 mg
- Protein 9 g

Strawberry Cheesecake Tarts

Prep Time: 15 minutes

Cooking Time: 35 minutes

Serving: 8

Ingredients:

Crust

- 2 cups almond flour
- 1/4 cup + 1 tbsp granulated Swerve
- 3 oz butter

Cheesecake filling

- 1 cup cream cheese
- 1/2 cup heavy whipping cream
- 1/4 cup + 1 tbsp confectioners Swerve
- 1/2 tsp sugar-free vanilla essence

Berry topping

- 1 cup strawberries
- 1 tsp granulated Swerve
- 1/4 tsp sugar-free vanilla essence

Method:

1. Let your oven preheat at 350 degrees F.
2. Mix almond meal with melted butter and sweetener in a bowl to form a coarse mixture.
3. Grease 6 mini tart pans and divides the crust mixture into the tart pans.
4. Poke some holes in each crust then bake them for 15 minutes.
5. Allow the crust to cool at room temperature.

6. Toss strawberries pieces with vanilla and sweetener in a bowl then spread them in a baking tray.
7. Bake the berries for 20 minutes then allow them to cool.
8. Beat cream cheese with vanilla, and sweetener in an electric mixer until fluffy.
9. Stir in cream and continue beating until creamy.
10. Pass one-half of the strawberries through a sieve to remove all the seeds.
11. Add this puree to the cream cheese mixture and mix gently to make swirls.
12. Divide this mixture into the tart crusts.
13. Refrigerate the tarts for 1 hour.
14. Top them with remaining berries.
15. Serve.

Nutritional Information per Serving:

- Calories 285
- Total Fat 27.3 g
- Saturated Fat 14.5 g
- Cholesterol 175 mg
- Total Carbs 3.5 g
- Sugar 0.4 g
- Fiber 0.9 g
- Sodium 165 mg
- Potassium 83 mg
- Protein 7.2 g

Cranberry Curd Tart

Prep Time: 15 minutes

Cooking Time: 25 minutes

Serving: 4

Ingredients:

Shortbread Tart Crust

- 1 cup blanched superfine almond flour
- 4 tablespoons salted butter
- 1 tablespoon Swerve
- 1 teaspoon vanilla

Keto Cranberry Curd

- 2-1/2cups cranberries
- ½ cup of water
- 6tablespoons salted butter
- ¼ cup Swerve
- 4 egg yolks
- ½ teaspoon vanilla

Method:

Keto Shortbread Tart Crust

1. Let your oven preheat at 350 degrees F. Grease an 8-inch tart pan.
2. Beat all the ingredients for the crust in an electric mixer to form a smooth dough.
3. Spread this dough in the greased tart pan.
4. Poke some holes in the crust and bake it for 15 minutes.
5. Set it aside to cool until filling is ready.

Keto Cranberry Curd

6. Boil cranberries with water in a saucepan then reduce the heat to a simmer.

7. Allow it to cool for 5 minutes while smashing the cranberries using a wooden spoon.
8. Pass this berry mixture through a sieve to remove the seeds.
9. This will give 1 cup cranberry puree.
10. Heat this puree in a saucepan then add salt, sweetener, and butter.
11. Mix well then remove it from the heat.
12. Once cooled, whisk in vanilla and egg yolks. Mix well until smooth.
13. Pour this filling in the baked crust.
14. Refrigerate them for 30 minutes.
15. Serve.

Nutritional Information per Serving:

- Calories 215
- Total Fat 20 g
- Saturated Fat 7 g
- Cholesterol 38 mg
- Total Carbs 8 g
- Sugar 1 g
- Fiber 6 g
- Sodium 12 mg
- Potassium 30 mg
- Protein 5 g

Chapter 7: Cookie Recipes

Double-Chocolate Keto Cookies

Prep Time: 10 minutes

Cooking Time: 12 minutes

Serving: 8

Ingredients:

- ¾ cup 2 tablespoons almond flour
- 1 tablespoon gelatine, grass-fed
- ½ teaspoon baking soda
- ½ teaspoon salt
- ¼ cup butter, unsalted, softened
- 3 tablespoons cocoa powder
- ½ teaspoon vanilla essence
- ¼ cup almond butter
- ½ cup granulated erythritol
- 1 large egg, room temperature
- ⅓ cup sugar free dark-chocolate, diced

Method:

1. Let your oven preheat at 350 degrees F. layer 2 baking trays with wax paper.
2. Mix almond flour with gelatin, baking soda, salt and cocoa powder in a suitable bowl.
3. Beat butter with sweetener and almond butter in an electric mixer.
4. Add egg and vanilla while beating the mixture.
5. Stir in almond flour mixture and mix well to form a dough.
6. Fold chocolate chunks then make 1-inch balls out of it.
7. Place these balls in the baking trays.
8. Press each ball into ½ inch thick cookie.

9. Bake these cookies for 12 minutes.
10. Allow them to cool at room temperature.
11. Serve.

Nutritional Information per Serving:

- Calories 198
- Total Fat 19.2 g
- Saturated Fat 11.5 g
- Cholesterol 123 mg
- Total Carbs 4.5 g
- Sugar 3.3 g
- Fiber 0.3 g
- Sodium 142 mg
- Potassium 34 mg
- Protein 3.4 g

Almond Butter Brownie Cookies

Prep Time: 10 minutes

Cooking Time: 12 minutes

Serving: 6

Ingredients:

- 1 cup almond butter
- 1/4 cup sugar free chocolate chips
- 1 large egg
- 4 tbsp sugar free cocoa powder
- 1/2 cup granulated erythritol
- 3 tbsp almond milk

Method:

1. Let the oven preheat at 350 degrees F.
2. Combine almond butter, egg, cocoa powder and sweetener in a suitable bowl.
3. Add 3 tbsp almond milk and mix well to make a soft dough.
4. Fold in chocolate chips then make small balls out of it.
5. Place these balls in the baking sheets and press them in thick cookies.
6. Bake these cookies for 12 minutes in the preheated oven.
7. Allow them to cool then serve.

Nutritional Information per Serving:

- Calories 288
- Total Fat 25.3 g
- Saturated Fat 6.7 g
- Cholesterol 23 mg
- Total Carbs 9.6 g
- Sugar 0.1 g
- Fiber 3.8 g
- Sodium 74 mg

- Potassium 3 mg
- Protein 7.6 g

Almond Cinnamon Butter Cookies

Prep Time: 15 minutes

Cooking Time: 15 minutes

Serving: 8

Ingredients:

- 1/2 cup butter, softened
- 2 cups blanched almond flour
- 1 egg
- 1/2 cup swerve
- 1 teaspoon vanilla essence
- 1 teaspoon cinnamon ground

Method:

1. Let your oven preheat at 350 degrees F. Layer a baking sheet with wax paper.
2. Toss almond flour with egg, butter, cinnamon, vanilla and swerve in a bowl.
3. Make 1-inch balls out of it and place them in a baking sheet.
4. Press them into cookies and make a criss-cross pattern over each cookie using a fork.
5. Bake them for 15 minutes until golden.
6. Allow them to cool.
7. Serve.

Nutritional Information per Serving:

- Calories 192
- Total Fat 17.44 g
- Saturated Fat 11.5 g
- Cholesterol 125 mg
- Total Carbs 2.2 g
- Sugar 1.4 g
- Fiber 2.1 g
- Sodium 135 mg

- Potassium 53 mg
- Protein 4.7 g

Cream Cheese Chocolate Cookies

Prep Time: 10 minutes

Cooking Time: 20 minutes

Serving: 6

Ingredients:

- 1/4 cup of cocoa powder
- 1 cup of coconut flour
- 2 ounces of baking chocolate
- 1 tsp of vanilla essence
- 2 teaspoons of baking powder
- 1/4 teaspoon sea salt
- ½ cup butter, unsalted softened
- 8 ounces cream cheese
- 1 cup swerve
- 1 tsp instant espresso coffee
- 4 eggs

Chocolate Icing

- A ¼ cup of butter, unsalted
- 1 tsp of MCT oil or coconut oil
- 1/2 cup swerve
- 2-ounce baking chocolate
- ½ tsp instant coffee powder
- Pinch of sea salt

Method:

Cookie Dough

1. Let your oven preheat at 350 degrees F.
2. Melt chocolate in a bowl by heating in the microwave for 20 seconds.

3. Beat cream cheese with vanilla essence, butter, and sweetener in an electric mixer.
4. Continue beating while adding eggs.
5. Add melted chocolate and mix well.
6. Stir in all the dry ingredients and mix again to form a cookie dough.

Chocolate Icing

7. Melt butter with chocolate in a bowl by heating in the microwave for 10 seconds.
8. Stir in sweetener, coconut oil, salt, and coffee. Mix well.

Baking

9. Divide the cookie dough into flat cookies and place them in a cookie sheet lined with wax paper.
10. Bake them for 20 minutes then allow them to cool.
11. Once cooled, top the cookies with prepared icing.
12. Serve after 5 minutes.

Nutritional Information per Serving:

- Calories 77.88
- Total Fat 7.13 g
- Saturated Fat 4.5 g
- Cholesterol 15 mg
- Total Carbs 0.8 g
- Sugar 0.2 g
- Fiber 0.3 g
- Sodium 15 mg
- Potassium 33 mg
- Protein 2.3 g

Keto Oreos

Prep Time: 15 minutes

Cooking Time: 12 minutes

Serving: 6

Ingredients:

Cookies

- 1/4 teaspoon salt
- 4 tablespoons cocoa powder
- 1 egg
- 3 tablespoons coconut flour
- 2 1/4 cups almond flour
- 1/2 teaspoon xanthan gum
- 1/2 cup swerve
- 1 teaspoons baking powder
- 1/2 cup butter, softened
- 1 teaspoon vanilla essence

Filling

- 2 tablespoons butter
- 4 oz. cream cheese, softened
- 1/2 teaspoons vanilla essence
- 1/2 cup powdered Swerve

Method:

1. Let your oven preheat at 350 degrees F.
2. Toss all the dry ingredients in a suitably sized bowl.
3. Beat cream with swerve and butter in an electric mixer until fluffy for 2 minutes.
4. Add vanilla and egg while mixing the mixture.
5. Stir in dry ingredients and mix thoroughly.

6. Spread this dough into 1/8-inch-thick sheet between two wax paper.
7. Cut the dough into cookies using a cookie cutter.
8. Place the cookies in the baking sheet lined with wax paper.
9. Bake them for 12 minutes then allow them to cool.

To make the filling

10. Meanwhile, beat cream with butter, vanilla and cream cheese in a mixer.
11. Spread the cream filling on top of half of the biscuits.
12. Place the remaining biscuits over the filling.
13. Serve.

Nutritional Information per Serving:

- Calories 114
- Total Fat 9.6 g
- Saturated Fat 4.5 g
- Cholesterol 10 mg
- Total Carbs 3.1 g
- Sugar 1.4 g
- Fiber 1.5 g
- Sodium 155 mg
- Potassium 93 mg
- Protein 3.5 g

Pecan Snowball Cookies

Prep Time: 10 minutes

Cooking Time: 15 minutes

Serving: 8

Ingredients:

- 8 tbsp butter
- 1 1/2 cup almond flour
- 1 cup pecans, chopped
- 1/2 cup Swerve
- 1 tsp vanilla essence
- 1/2 tsp vanilla liquid stevia
- 1/4 tsp salt
- extra confectioners to roll balls in

Method:

1. Let your oven preheat at 350 degrees F.
2. Put all the dough ingredients in a food processor and blend well to form a dough ball.
3. Layer a baking sheet with parchment paper.
4. Add cookie batter to the baking sheet scoop by scoop to make 24 separate mounds.
5. Spread these mounds into flat cookies.
6. Freeze them for 30 minutes then bake them for 15 minutes.
7. Allow them to cool then roll the cookies in the swerve confectioners.
8. Serve.

Nutritional Information per Serving:

- Calories 252
- Total Fat 17.3 g
- Saturated Fat 11.5 g
- Cholesterol 141 mg

- Total Carbs 7.2 g
- Sugar 0.3 g
- Fiber 1.4 g
- Sodium 153 mg
- Potassium 73 mg
- Protein 5.2 g

Pumpkin Butter Cookies

Prep Time: 15 minutes

Cooking Time: 25 minutes

Serving: 8

Ingredients:

- ¼ cup pumpkin puree
- 1 large egg
- 1 cup almond flour
- ½ tsp baking powder
- ½ tsp pumpkin pie spice
- ½ tsp vanilla essence
- ¼ cup butter
- ¼ cup powdered erythritol
- ¼ cup Lily's chocolate chips, dark

Method:

1. Let your oven preheat at 350 degrees F.
2. Beat pumpkin puree with butter in an electric mixer.
3. Add egg, baking powder, vanilla essence, erythritol, and almond flour. Mix well.
4. Once smooth fold in chocolate chips and mix gently.
5. Divide this dough into equal size balls and flatten these balls into cookies.
6. Bake them for 25 minutes in the cookie tray until golden.
7. Allow them to cool then serve.
8. Enjoy.

Nutritional Information per Serving:

- Calories 195
- Total Fat 14.3 g
- Saturated Fat 10.5 g
- Cholesterol 175 mg

- Total Carbs 4.5 g
- Sugar 0.5 g
- Fiber 0.3 g
- Sodium 125 mg
- Potassium 83 mg
- Protein 3.2 g

Hazelnut Flour Cookies

Prep Time: 10 minutes

Cooking Time: 25 minutes

Serving: 6

Ingredients:

- 1 cup hazelnut meal ground
- 2 egg whites
- 1 tbsp powdered erythritol
- 10 drops vanilla stevia glycerite
- 1 tsp vanilla
- crushed hazelnuts to decorate

Method:

1. Swiftly beat egg whites in an electric mixer until they form peaks.
2. Gently fold in hazelnut meal, vanilla, stevia, and erythritol.
3. Mix well then drop the dough scoop by scoop over a baking sheet lined with parchment paper.
4. Flatten each scoop into flat cookies and bake them for 25 minutes at 320 degrees F.
5. Allow them to cool then serve.
6. Enjoy.

Nutritional Information per Serving:

- Calories 151
- Total Fat 14.7 g
- Saturated Fat 1.5 g
- Cholesterol 13 mg
- Total Carbs 1.5 g
- Sugar 0.3 g
- Fiber 0.1 g
- Sodium 53 mg

- Potassium 131 mg
- Protein 0.8 g

Chapter8: Candy and Confections

Chocolate Kisses Candy

Prep Time: 15 minutes

Cooking Time: 0 minute

Serving: 12

Ingredients:

- 1 oz cocoa butter
- 1/2 teaspoon vanilla essence
- 4 oz sugar free baking chocolate
- 1/8 teaspoon stevia powder
- 3 tablespoons swerve powder

Method:

1. Melt chocolate with cocoa butter and sweetener in a bowl by heating in a microwave.
2. Stir in vanilla essences and stevia and mix well.
3. Pour this mixture into candy molds.
4. Freeze the candies until set.
5. Serve after removing them from the molds.

Nutritional Information per Serving:

- Calories 261
- Total Fat 27.1 g
- Saturated Fat 23.4 g
- Cholesterol 0 mg
- Total Carbs 6.1 g
- Sugar 2.1 g
- Fiber 3.9 g
- Sodium 10 mg

- Potassium 57 mg
- Protein 1.8 g

Lemon Drop Gummies

Prep Time: 15 minutes

Cooking Time: 0 minute

Serving: 12

Ingredients:

- 1/4 cup fresh lemon juice
- 1 tablespoon water
- 2 tablespoons gelatine powder
- 2 tablespoons erythritol or stevia, to taste

Method:

1. Let the lemon juice and water warm up in a saucepan.
2. Gradually stir in erythritol and gelatine powder. Mix well.
3. Divide the mixture into silicone molds.
4. Refrigerate them for 2 hours until set.
5. Serve after removing them from the molds.

Nutritional Information per Serving:

- Calories 139
- Total Fat 4.6 g
- Saturated Fat 0.5 g
- Cholesterol 1.2 mg
- Total Carbs 7.5 g
- Sugar 6.3 g
- Fiber 0.6 g
- Sodium 83 mg
- Potassium 113 mg
- Protein 3.8 g

Coconut Blueberry Gummies

Prep Time: 15 minutes

Cooking Time: 0 minute

Serving: 8

Ingredients:

- 2 cups of coconut milk
- A ¼ cup of blueberry juice
- ¼ cup gelatine, grass fed

Method:

1. Mix gelatine with blueberry juice in a bowl.
2. Heat coconut milk in a saucepan over medium heat.
3. Whisk in gelatine mixture and stir cook until dissolved.
4. Remove the pan from the heat then divide the mixture into silicone molds.
5. Refrigerate them for 2 hours to set.
6. Serve after removing them from the molds.

Nutritional Information per Serving:

- Calories 200
- Total Fat 21.1 g
- Saturated Fat 19.5 g
- Cholesterol 14.2 mg
- Total Carbs 1.1 g
- Sugar 1.3 g
- Fiber 0.4 g
- Sodium 46 mg
- Potassium 145 mg
- Protein 0.4 g

White Chocolate Fat Bombs

Prep Time: 15 minutes

Cooking Time: 0 minute

Serving: 8

Ingredients:

- 6 tablespoons cacao butter, melted
- 1 cup coconut cream
- 4 teaspoons vanilla essence
- 3 tablespoons College Latin
- Pinch of salt
- 1/2 cup water
- 3 tablespoons granulated swerve

Method:

1. Dissolve gelatin in water in a small bowl and let it sit for 5 minutes.
2. Combine all the remaining ingredients in a saucepan on low heat while stirring.
3. Add gelatine and mix well until dissolved.
4. Divide the mixture into the silicone molds.
5. Refrigerate them for 1 hour.
6. Serve after removing them from the molds.

Nutritional Information per Serving:

- Calories 136
- Total Fat 10.7 g
- Saturated Fat 0.5 g
- Cholesterol 4 mg
- Total Carbs 1.2 g
- Sugar 1.4 g
- Fiber 0 g
- Sodium 45 mg

- Potassium 31 mg
- Protein 0. g

Butter Mints

Prep Time: 15 minutes

Cooking Time: 5 minutes

Serving: 4

Ingredients:

- 8 ounces butter
- 1/4 cup raw honey
- 1 teaspoon vanilla essence
- 1/2 teaspoon peppermint extract
- Salt to taste, if using butter, unsalted

Method:

1. Blend butter with salt, peppermint extract and vanilla essence in a food processor.
2. Spread the parchment paper on a baking tray.
3. Add the butter mixture over baking tray dollop by dollop.
4. Place these butter bites in the freezer for 1 hour.
5. Serve.

Nutritional Information per Serving:

- Calories 91
- Total Fat 4.7 g
- Saturated Fat 0.8 g
- Cholesterol 11 mg
- Total Carbs 0 g
- Sugar 0.2 g
- Fiber 0.5 g
- Sodium 43 mg
- Potassium 181 mg
- Protein 2 g

Peppermint Frost Mints

Prep Time: 15 minutes

Cooking Time: 5 minutes

Serving: 4

Ingredients:

- 1 cup xylitol
- 4 drops peppermint extract

Method:

1. Cook xylitol in a saucepan over low heat for 5 minutes to melt.
2. Meanwhile, layer a jelly roll pan with wax paper.
3. Allow the xylitol to cool for 10 minutes then add peppermint extract.
4. Mix well then spread this mixture over a baking tray lined with parchment paper.
5. Let it sit overnight to dry the mixture.
6. Break it into bite-sized pieces.
7. Serve.

Nutritional Information per Serving:

- Calories 38
- Total Fat 0.6 g
- Saturated Fat 0 g
- Cholesterol 0 mg
- Total Carbs 0 g
- Sugar 0 g
- Fiber 0 g
- Sodium 33 mg
- Potassium 1 mg
- Protein 9 g

Peppermint Marshmallows

Prep Time: 15 minutes

Cooking Time: 20 minutes

Serving: 8

Ingredients:

- 1 cup water, divided
- 2 1/2 tbsp gelatine, grass fed
- 2/3 cup Swerve powder
- 1/8 tsp cream of tartar
- 2/3 cup Bocha Sweet
- Pinch salt
- 1 tsp peppermint extract

Method:

1. Layer an 8-inch pan with parchment paper and grease it with cooking spray.
2. Mix half of the water-gelatin in a small bowl. Let it sit for 5 minutes.
3. Heat the remaining water with sweetener in a saucepan.
4. Add salt, gelatine, and cream of tartar. Mix well to dissolve the sweetener.
5. Cook the mixture to reach at 240 degrees F then turn off the heat.
6. Beat this hot syrup in a stand mixer on low speed until it thickens, for about 15 minutes.
7. Spread this mixture in a baking pan evenly.
8. Refrigerate it for 4 hours.
9. Break into pieces then serve.

Nutritional Information per Serving:

- Calories 76
- Total Fat 7.2 g
- Saturated Fat 6.4 g
- Cholesterol 0 mg

- Total Carbs 2g
- Sugar 1 g
- Fiber 0.7 g
- Sodium 8 mg
- Potassium 88 mg
- Protein 2.2 g

White Chocolate Bark

Prep Time: 10 minutes

Cooking Time: 0 minute

Serving: 6

Ingredients:

- 3/4 cup cacao butter melted
- 1/4 cup cashew butter
- 1/4 cup coconut butter
- 1/4 cup coconut cream
- 3 tbsp liquid coconut nectar
- 2 tsp vanilla essence
- Pinch sea salt

Method:

1. Blend melted cacao butter with remaining ingredients in a blender until smooth.
2. Spread this mixture in a baking pan into a thin layer.
3. Freeze it for 2 hours.
4. Break into pieces then serve.

Nutritional Information per Serving:

- Calories 193
- Total Fat 20 g
- Saturated Fat 13.2 g
- Cholesterol 10 mg
- Total Carbs 2.5 g
- Sugar 1 g
- Sodium 8 mg
- Potassium 88 mg
- Protein 2.2 g

Chapter9: Frozen Desserts

Chocolate Avocado Ice Cream

Prep Time: 15 minutes

Cooking Time: 0 minute

Serving: 4

Ingredients:

- 1/8 teaspoon stevia powder
- 1/3 cup allulose powder
- 1 cup coconut milk
- 2 avocados, pitted and peeled
- 1/2 cup coconut cream
- 1/2 cup cocoa powder
- 2 teaspoons vanilla essence

Method:

1. Add avocado flesh to the food processor along with all other ingredients.
2. Transfer this mixture in the ice cream machine and churn it as per the machine's instructions.
3. Allow it to freeze until it is ready to serve.
4. Enjoy.

Nutritional Information per Serving:

- Calories 173
- Total Fat 13 g
- Saturated Fat 10.1 g
- Cholesterol 12 mg
- Total Carbs 7.5 g
- Sugar 1.2 g

- Fiber 0.6 g
- Sodium 67 mg
- Potassium 91 mg
- Protein 3.2 g

Mix Berry Popsicles

Prep Time: 15 minutes

Cooking Time: 0 minute

Serving: 4

Ingredients:

- 5 oz cream cheese
- 1/4 cup full-fat coconut milk
- 3 tbsp yogurt
- 1/4 cup powdered erythritol
- 2 tbsp shredded coconut
- 1 tsp chia seeds
- 1/4 cup frozen strawberries
- 1/4 cup frozen blueberries
- 1/4 cup frozen blackberries
- 1/2 tsp MCT oil

Method:

1. First blend all the popsicle ingredients in a blender except the berries.
2. Now add berries and pulse for 2 seconds to break the berries into pieces.
3. Pour this mixture into suitable popsicle molds and insert ice cream sticks in it.
4. Freeze them for 2 hours or more.
5. Remove the popsicles from the molds.
6. Serve.

Nutritional Information per Serving:

- Calories 197
- Total Fat 19.2 g
- Saturated Fat 10.1 g
- Cholesterol 11 mg
- Total Carbs 7.3 g

- Sugar 1.2 g
- Fiber 0.8 g
- Sodium 78 mg
- Potassium 109 mg
- Protein 4.2 g

Blueberry Lemon Cheesecake

Prep Time: 15 minutes

Cooking Time: 0 minute

Serving: 6

Ingredients:

- 8 oz cream cheese
- 1/2 cup heavy whipping cream
- 1/4 cup sour cream
- 1/2 cup swerve confectioner
- 3 ounces blueberries
- 1 tsp vanilla essence
- 15 drops liquid stevia
- 1 lemon zest
- 1 lemon juice
- 6 popsicle silicone molds

Method:

1. Beat the sour cream with heavy cream in a mixer.
2. Whisk in lemon zest, juice, stevia, swerve and vanilla essence.
3. Add berries and mix well while mashing the berries with a spoon.
4. Pour this mixture into suitable popsicle molds and insert ice cream sticks in it.
5. Freeze them for 6 hours or more.
6. Remove the popsicles from the molds.
7. Serve.

Nutritional Information per Serving:

- Calories 213
- Total Fat 19 g
- Saturated Fat 15.2 g
- Cholesterol 13 mg

- Total Carbs 5.5 g
- Sugar 1.3 g
- Fiber 0.5 g
- Sodium 52 mg
- Potassium 87 mg
- Protein 6.1 g

Fudge Popsicles

Prep Time: 15 minutes

Cooking Time: 0 minute

Serving: 4

Ingredients:

- 1 3/4 cup heavy cream
- 2 1/2 ounces sugar free chocolate, chopped
- 1/3 cup erythritol blend
- 2 large eggs
- 3/4 cup almond milk
- 1 teaspoon vanilla essence

Method:

1. Mix heavy cream with chocolate, eggs, and sweetener in a saucepan.
2. Let this mixture simmer on low heat then remove it instantly.
3. Stir in vanilla essence and almond milk. Mix well.
4. Pour this mixture into suitable popsicle molds and insert ice cream sticks in it.
5. Freeze them for 5 hours or more.
6. Remove the popsicles from the molds.
7. Serve.

Nutritional Information per Serving:

- Calories 117
- Total Fat 21.2 g
- Saturated Fat 10.4 g
- Cholesterol 19.7 mg
- Total Carbs 7.3 g
- Sugar 3.4 g
- Fiber 2 g
- Sodium 104 mg

- Potassium 196 mg
- Protein 8.1 g

Blueberry Mint Popsicles

Prep Time: 15 minutes

Cooking Time: 20 minutes

Serving: 2

Ingredients:

- 1 can coconut milk
- 1/2 cup blueberries
- 1/2-ounce lime juice
- 2 tbsp mint leaves

Method:

1. Let coconut milk simmer in a saucepan for 5 minutes with mint leaves.
2. Remove it from the heat then strain and allow it to cool.
3. Heat blueberries with lime juice in a saucepan over low, medium heat for 5 minutes.
4. Allow this berry compote to cool at room temperature.
5. Divide the coconut milk into the popsicle molds.
6. Freeze them for 30 minutes then remove the molds from the freezer.
7. Add berry compote to each mold and make swirls using a stick.
8. Insert ice cream sticks into the molds and freeze again for 2 hours or more.
9. Serve.

Nutritional Information per Serving:

- Calories 113
- Total Fat 9 g
- Saturated Fat 0.2 g
- Cholesterol 1.7 mg
- Total Carbs 6.5 g
- Sugar 1.8 g
- Fiber 0.7 g

- Sodium 134 mg
- Potassium 123 mg
- Protein 7.5 g

Raspberry Lemon Popsicles

Prep Time: 15 minutes

Cooking Time: 0 minute

Serving: 2

Ingredients:

- 1 cup lemon juice
- 2 cups water
- 3 to 5 doonks of stevia
- ½ cup frozen raspberries, roughly chopped

Method:

1. Divide the chopped berries into popsicle molds.
2. Mix lemon juice with stevia, and water in a bowl.
3. Divide this mixture into the popsicle molds and insert the ice cream sticks in it.
4. Freeze them for about 4 hours or more.
5. Serve after removing from the molds.
6. Enjoy.

Nutritional Information per Serving:

- Calories 101
- Total Fat 15.5 g
- Saturated Fat 4.5 g
- Cholesterol 12 mg
- Total Carbs 4.4 g
- Sugar 1.2 g
- Fiber 0.3 g
- Sodium 18 mg
- Potassium 128 mg
- Protein 4.8 g

Berries and Cream Popsicles

Prep Time: 15 minutes

Cooking Time: 0 minute

Serving: 4

Ingredients:

- 8 ounces of cream cheese softened
- 2 cups of heavy whipping cream
- 1 tablespoon of lemon juice
- 1/4 cup of sour cream
- 1 1/2 cups of fresh sliced strawberries
- 1 cup of fresh blueberries
- 3/4 cup of swerve

Method:

1. Blend cream cheese with lemon juice, sour cream, and heavy cream in a food processor until smooth.
2. Add ½ cup blueberries, 1 cup strawberries, and sweetener.
3. Blender well until smooth.
4. Add remaining berries to the bottom of each popsicle mold.
5. Divide the cream cheese mixture into these molds.
6. Insert the ice cream stick into each mold.
7. Freeze them for about 4 hours or more.
8. Serve after removing from the molds.
9. Enjoy.

Nutritional Information per Serving:

- Calories 266
- Total Fat 25.7 g
- Saturated Fat 1.2 g
- Cholesterol 41 mg

- Total Carbs 9.7 g
- Sugar 1.2 g
- Fiber 0.5 g
- Sodium 18 mg
- Potassium 78 mg
- Protein 2.6 g

Chocolate Peanut Butter Popsicles

Prep Time: 15 minutes

Cooking Time: 0 minute

Serving: 4

Ingredients:

- 1/2 cup peanut butter
- 1 tsp liquid stevia
- 1.5 cups almond milk
- 1 cup heavy whipping cream
- 1/4 cup cocoa powder sugar free

Method:

1. Beat all the ingredients together in a food processor until smooth.
2. Divide this mixture into the popsicle molds and insert the ice cream sticks in it.
3. Freeze them for about 4 hours or more.
4. Serve after removing from the molds.
5. Enjoy.

Nutritional Information per Serving:

- Calories 147
- Total Fat 11 g
- Saturated Fat 10.1 g
- Cholesterol 10 mg
- Total Carbs 4.2 g
- Sugar 2 g
- Fiber 0.4 g
- Sodium 91 mg
- Potassium 48 mg
- Protein 3.2 g

Chapter 10: Custard or Mousse Recipes

Zesty Keto custard

Prep Time: 15 minutes

Cooking Time: 0 minute

Serving: 2

Ingredients:

- 2 tsp xylitol or natvia
- 4 egg yolks
- ¼ tsp ground vanilla bean
- ¾ cup whipping/pouring cream
- 1 tsp xanthan gum

Optional flavors

- 1 tsp raw cacao
- 1/2 tsp lemon zest

Method:

1. Beat sweetener with egg yolks, xanthan gum, vanilla until pale in color.
2. Boil cream in a saucepan then whisk in yolk mixture gradually while stirring.
3. Remove the cooked custard from the heat and continue stirring for 1 minute.
4. Allow it to cool then garnish with cocoa or lemon zest.
5. Enjoy.

Nutritional Information per Serving:

- Calories 243
- Total Fat 21 g
- Saturated Fat 18.2 g
- Cholesterol 121 mg

- Total Carbs 7.3 g
- Sugar 0.9 g
- Fiber 0.1 g
- Sodium 34 mg
- Potassium 181 mg
- Protein 4.3 g

Keto Lemon Custard

Prep Time: 15 minutes

Cooking Time: 50 minutes

Serving: 2

Ingredients:

- 2 cup heavy cream or 2 cups coconut milk
- 2 tablespoons lemon zest about 2 lemons
- 6 large eggs
- sliced lemons for topping optional
- Sweetener
- 1 cup swerve granulated works best

Method:

1. Let your oven preheat at 300 degrees F.
2. Blend all the ingredients in a bowl using a hand mixer for 1 minute.
3. Divide this mixture into two half-cup ramekins.
4. Set these ramekins in a baking pan.
5. Add enough hot water to the pan to cover the ¾ of the ramekins.
6. Bake them for 50 minutes.
7. Allow the ramekins to cool at room temperature then refrigerate for 2 hours.
8. Garnish with lemon slices.
9. Enjoy.

Nutritional Information per Serving:

- Calories 183
- Total Fat 15 g
- Saturated Fat 12.1 g
- Cholesterol 11 mg
- Total Carbs 6.2 g
- Sugar 1.6 g

- Fiber 0.8 g
- Sodium 31 mg
- Potassium 91 mg
- Protein 4.5 g

Mocha Custards

Prep Time: 15 minutes

Cooking Time: 5 minutes

Serving: 5

Ingredients:

- 1/2 cups heavy cream
- 1/4 cups coffee strong black
- 3 egg yolks
- 1 tbsp granulated sweetener of choice or more, to your taste
- 1.8 oz 90% dark chocolate

Method:

1. Warm up the cream in a saucepan with chocolate pieces and coffee on a simmer.
2. Then remove them from heat.
3. Beat egg yolks with sweetener in a mixer until fluffy and pale in color.
4. Gradually pour this mixture into the cream mixture while mixing gently.
5. Return the saucepan to low heat and stir cook until it thickens.
6. Divide into cups and refrigerate until custard is set.
7. Serve.

Nutritional Information per Serving:

- Calories 388
- Total Fat 31 g
- Saturated Fat 12.2 g
- Cholesterol 101 mg
- Total Carbs 3 g
- Sugar 1.3 g
- Sodium 54 mg
- Potassium 94 mg
- Protein 5 g

Blueberry Creme Brulee

Prep Time: 15 minutes

Cooking Time: 50 minutes

Serving: 4

Ingredients:

Brûlée

- 5 egg yolks
- 1 tsp vanilla essence
- 1/8 tsp salt
- 1/3 cup granulated swerve
- 2 cups heavy cream

filling

- 1/3 cup water
- 1/3 cup granulated swerve
- 1 cup fresh blueberries

Method:

Filling

1. Mix water, swerve and blueberries in a cooking pot over medium-high heat.
2. Let it boil then cook it on a simmer until it thickens.
3. Remove the blupan from the heat and allow it to cool.

Brulee

4. Warm heavy cream with salt in a cooking pan over medium heat on low heat until it bubbles.
5. Remove it from the heat then add vanilla.
6. Meanwhile, beat egg yolks with swerve in an electric mixer until creamy.
7. Add 1/3 cream into egg yolks mixture and mix well.

8. Return this mixture to the cream while mixing well.

Assemble

9. Let your oven preheat at 350 degrees F.
10. Add 2 tbsps blueberry sauce in each ramekin.
11. Divide the custard over this filling in each ramekin.
12. Bake them for 40 minutes in the preheated oven.
13. Allow it to cool then refrigerate for 2 hours or more.
14. Serve.

Nutritional Information per Serving:

- Calories 153
- Total Fat 13 g
- Saturated Fat 9.2 g
- Cholesterol 6.5 mg
- Total Carbs 4.5 g
- Sugar 1.4 g
- Fiber 0.4 g
- Sodium 81 mg
- Potassium 58 mg
- Protein 5.8 g

Peanut Butter Mousse

Prep Time: 5 minutes

Cooking Time: 0 minute

Serving: 2

Ingredients:

- ½ cup heavy whipping cream
- 4 oz cream cheese (softened)
- 1/4 cup peanut butter
- 1/4 cup powdered Swerve Sweetener
- ½ tsp vanilla essence

Method:

1. Beat ½ cup cream in a mixer until it forms stiff peaks.
2. Take cream cheese in another bowl and blend it with peanut butter.
3. Add vanilla, salt, and sweetener while beating this mixture.
4. Fold in whipped cream and then divide this mixture into serving glasses.
5. Garnish with chocolate sauce.
6. Enjoy.

Nutritional Information per Serving:

- Calories 254
- Total Fat 09 g
- Saturated Fat 10.1 g
- Cholesterol 13 mg
- Total Carbs 7.5 g
- Sugar 1.2 g
- Fiber 0.8 g
- Sodium 179 mg
- Potassium 58 mg
- Protein 7.5 g

Chocolate Mousse Recipe

Prep Time: 15 minutes

Cooking Time: 0 minute

Serving: 4

Ingredients

- 1 1/4 cup Coconut Cream
- 1/4 cup Heavy Cream
- 2 tbsp Cocoa sugar free
- 3 tbsp Erythritol
- 1 tsp vanilla essence

Method:

1. Blend all the ingredients in a mixer on low speed until it is thick.
2. Divide the mousse in the ramekins.
3. Garnish as desired.
4. Serve.

Nutritional Information per Serving:

- Calories 265
- Total Fat 13 g
- Saturated Fat 10.2 g
- Cholesterol 09 mg
- Total Carbs 7.5 g
- Sugar 1.1 g
- Fiber 0.5 g
- Sodium 7.1 mg
- Potassium 68 mg
- Protein 5.2 g

Chocolate Mousse

Prep Time: 15 minutes

Cooking Time: 0 minute

Serving: 2

Ingredients:

- 1 cup heavy cream
- 2 tbsp sugar free cocoa powder
- 3 packets stevia, or 2tbsp granular sweetener
- 1 tsp vanilla essence

Method:

1. Beat all the ingredients in an electric mixer until it forms peaks.
2. Garnish with whipped cream.
3. Serve.

Nutritional Information per Serving:

- Calories 290
- Total Fat 21.5 g
- Saturated Fat 15.2 g
- Cholesterol 12.1 mg
- Total Carbs 6.5 g
- Sugar 1.2 g
- Fiber 0.4 g
- Sodium 9 mg
- Potassium 82 mg
- Protein 6.2 g

Cheesecake Mousse Fluff

Prep Time: 15 minutes

Cooking Time: 0 minute

Serving: 4

Ingredients:

- 1/3 cup erythritol powder
- 8 oz. cream cheese, room temperature
- 1/8 teaspoon stevia powder, if desired
- 1 1/2 teaspoons vanilla essence
- 1/4 teaspoon lemon extract
- 1 cup heavy whipping cream or regular heavy cream

Method:

1. Beat cream cheese in an electric mixer until smooth.
2. Whisk in lemon extract, vanilla, stevia, and erythritol. Mix well and set it aside.
3. Beat cream in the mixer until it forms peaks.
4. Slowly fold in cream cheese mixture. Continue beating until fluffy.
5. Refrigerate it for 2 hours.
6. Serve.

Nutritional Information per Serving:

- Calories 306
- Total Fat 30.8 g
- Saturated Fat 19.3 g
- Cholesterol 103 mg
- Total Carbs 4.6 g
- Sugar 0.3 g
- Sodium 179 mg
- Potassium 92 mg
- Protein 4.9 g

Conclusion

Following a health-oriented diet plan does not mean you need to ditch the variety and quality of the food. Even following a keto diet, now you can enjoy absolutely carb free food without compromising on taste, and aroma. Same can be said for ketogenic desserts now! As we have shared several new and delicious low carb dessert ideas in this cookbook. Whether you are craving for chocolate rich bars, gummies, creamy cakes or ice creams, this book brings the best of flavors through a range of varieties. Now you can get to enjoy all your favorite desserts in keto style.

27117313R00066

Printed in Great Britain
by Amazon